COOL CAVES

CONTENTS

make believe ideas

WHAT ARE CAVES?

Caves can be dark and dangerous places, but they are also fascinating. Short and wide caves are often found along coastlines and are known as sea caves. Long and narrow caves go deeper underground and can form huge cave systems. Most caves formed thousands or even millions of years ago.

Melissani Cave is a deep, lake-filled cave on Kefalonia Island in Greece. Guides lead visitors through the cave in rowboats.

Benagil Cave is a sea cave in Portugal. The sun shines through a hole in its roof, known as the "eye," lighting up the cave walls.

STALAGMITES AND STALACTITES

Stalagmites and **stalactites** are rock formations made from the minerals in dripping water. **Stalagmites** grow upward from the ground, while **stalactites** hang down like icicles from the ceiling of a cave.

stalactite

stalagmite

The Luray Caverns in Virginia have many **stalagmites** and **stalactites**. Iron in the local water has stained some of them an orange color.

The Marble Cathedral is a **glacial** lake cave in Chile. Over thousands of years, water carved the rock into smooth columns and caverns.

DID YOU KNOW?

The Jenolan Caves in Australia are the world's oldest-known caves. They are about 340 million years old—that's older than the first dinosaurs!

TYPES OF CAVES

Caves form in different ways. Wind, waves, and underground water can all carve out caves from rock. Caves form in other ways, too. Hot **lava** and freezing ice can also create cool caves.

SEA CAVE
The Blue Grotto in Italy is a sea cave with bright blue water. Sunlight shining into the cave makes the water look like it's glowing.

SOLUTIONAL CAVE
When underground water dissolves soft rock, it can create the most common type of cave—a **solutional cave**. These caves often have **stalagmites** and **stalactites**. The **stalactites** in Mammoth Cave, Kentucky, look like waterfalls. This one is called Frozen Niagara.

LAVA CAVE
About 500 years ago, a river of **molten lava** created the Nāhuku **Lava** Tube in Hawaii.

EOLIAN CAVE
Strong desert winds in the Carrizo Badlands in California carved out **eolian caves** from sandstone.

GLACIER CAVE
Tightly packed ice in the Vatnajökull **Glacier** Caves in Iceland looks like sparkling blue glass.

HOW DO CAVES FORM?

Water moving against rock is one of the most common ways in which caves form. Each time it happens, a little of the rock washes away. This process is called **erosion**. Over many years, waves and underground streams can carve huge caves in solid rock.

This sea cave near Auckland, New Zealand, floods with water every high tide but empties when the tide is out.

HOW SEA CAVES FORM

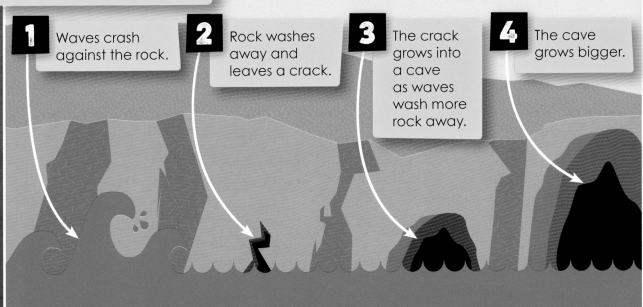

1 Waves crash against the rock.

2 Rock washes away and leaves a crack.

3 The crack grows into a cave as waves wash more rock away.

4 The cave grows bigger.

HOW STALACTITES AND STALAGMITES FORM

1 Water drips from the ceiling to the floor of the cave.

2 Minerals left by the water drips harden into icicle-shaped rocks called **stalactites**.

column

stalactite

stalagmite

3 Minerals left by the water drips on the cave floor harden into candle-shaped rocks called **stalagmites**.

4 **Stalactites** and **stalagmites** can join to form columns.

Caves in Xintai City, China

HOW SOLUTIONAL CAVES FORM

1 Water seeps through cracks in soft rock.

2 It dissolves some of the rock, making bigger gaps.

3 More water flows in, dissolving more rock and creating a cave.

7

UNDERGROUND RIVERS

Underground, or subterranean, rivers run below the Earth's surface. Many flow naturally through cave systems, creating some of the world's most unusual and challenging **habitats**.

Puerto Princesa Subterranean River in the Philippines flows under mountains and out to the ocean. Some of the creatures that live there can't be found anywhere else in the world.

Grjótagjá Cave in Iceland is a volcanic cave with a hot, **geothermal** river. It's so hot in places that swimming is forbidden!

A type of giant huntsman spider lives inside the cave.

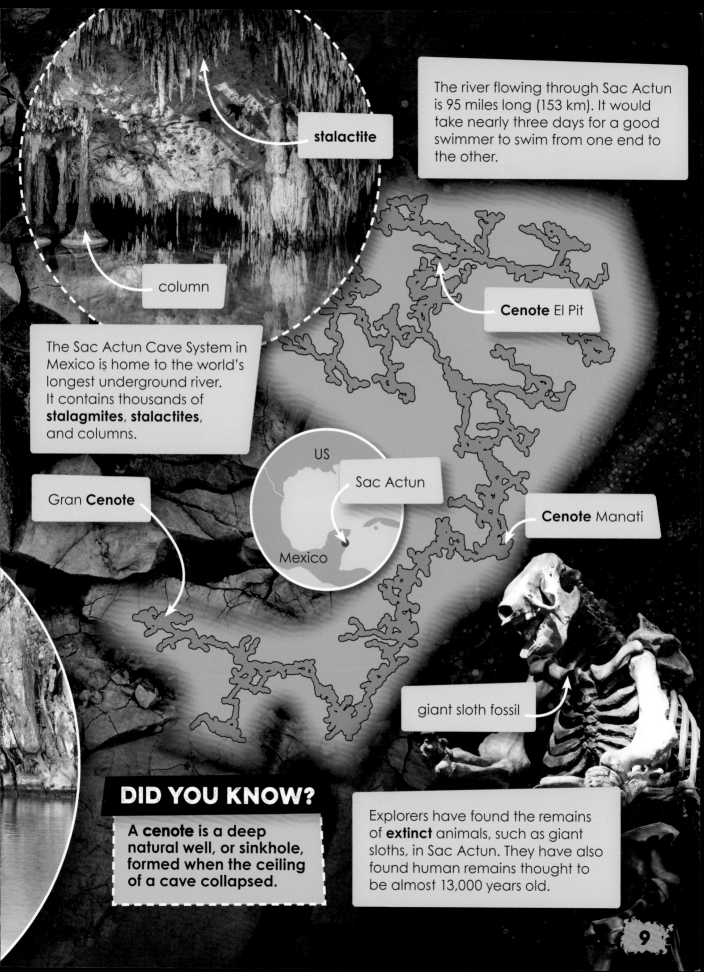

stalactite

column

The river flowing through Sac Actun is 95 miles long (153 km). It would take nearly three days for a good swimmer to swim from one end to the other.

Cenote El Pit

The Sac Actun Cave System in Mexico is home to the world's longest underground river. It contains thousands of **stalagmites**, **stalactites**, and columns.

US

Sac Actun

Mexico

Gran **Cenote**

Cenote Manati

giant sloth fossil

DID YOU KNOW?

A **cenote** is a deep natural well, or sinkhole, formed when the ceiling of a cave collapsed.

Explorers have found the remains of **extinct** animals, such as giant sloths, in Sac Actun. They have also found human remains thought to be almost 13,000 years old.

ICE CAVES

Ice caves are made in two ways. Some form in **glaciers** when water runs under or through the ice and melts it, leaving behind openings or tunnels. Other ice caves are rocky caverns that stay cold enough to contain ice much of the year.

SHAPE-SHIFTERS
Vatnajökull **Glacier** Caves in Iceland change size and shape every year as water carves new openings in the ice.

ICE GIANT

The World of the Ice Giants in Austria lives up to its big name, with a total length of more than 26 miles (42 km). That's about the same length as a marathon race!

FIRE AND ICE

Kamchatka Ice Cave in Russia formed when a hot-water spring flowed under the ice on a volcanic mountain. The thin, icy walls let sunlight shine through, creating rainbow-colored ice.

WINTER WONDERLAND

The Apostle Islands Caves in Wisconsin turn into icy wonderlands in winter. Lake water dripping through cracks in the cliffs freezes, creating giant icicles.

GIANT CAVES

Caves come in all shapes and sizes, but some of the most impressive are the biggest, the longest, and the deepest.

Hang Son Doong Cave, Vietnam

THE BIGGEST CAVE

Some of the caverns in Hang Son Doong Cave in Vietnam are big enough to hold a 40-story skyscraper. An underground jungle grows in parts of the cave where the roof has collapsed and sunlight shines in.

THE LONGEST CAVE

Mammoth Cave in Kentucky has more than 400 miles (644 km) of tunnels. It would take about 8 hours to drive the length of the cave.

Crystal Cave

MAMMOTH CAVE NATIONAL PARK

Frozen Niagara

Sand Cave

Canada

US

Mammoth Cave

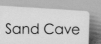

SUPER STALACTITE

Over thousands of years, a single continuous drip of water formed Europe's biggest **stalactite**. The Great **Stalactite** in Doolin Caves in Ireland weighs about 11 tons (10 tonnes). That's more than two elephants!

THE DEEPEST CAVE

To reach the bottom of Veryovkina Cave in Georgia, cave explorers, also known as **spelunkers**, must descend 7,257 feet (2,212 m). That's about the same distance as 21 soccer fields lined end to end.

FAMOUS CAVE RESCUE:
THAM LUANG

Caves are exciting places to explore, but they can be dangerous, too. In 2018, a junior soccer team and their coach were trapped in a cave in Thailand. Heavy rain had flooded the caves.

The junior soccer team, the Wild Boars, and their coach went into the caves after a training session.

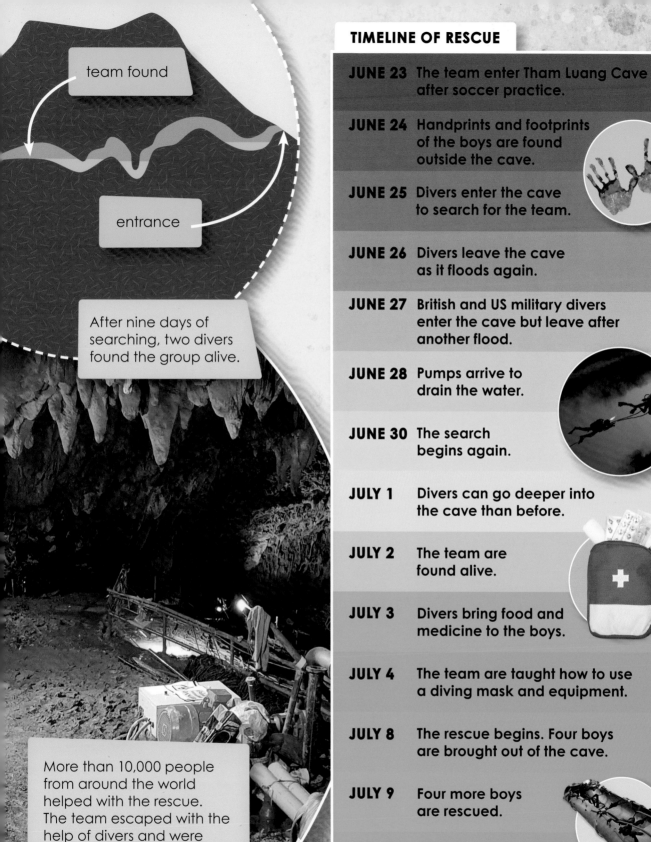

team found

entrance

After nine days of searching, two divers found the group alive.

More than 10,000 people from around the world helped with the rescue. The team escaped with the help of divers and were pulled over rocky sections of the tunnel on stretchers.

TIMELINE OF RESCUE

JUNE 23 The team enter Tham Luang Cave after soccer practice.

JUNE 24 Handprints and footprints of the boys are found outside the cave.

JUNE 25 Divers enter the cave to search for the team.

JUNE 26 Divers leave the cave as it floods again.

JUNE 27 British and US military divers enter the cave but leave after another flood.

JUNE 28 Pumps arrive to drain the water.

JUNE 30 The search begins again.

JULY 1 Divers can go deeper into the cave than before.

JULY 2 The team are found alive.

JULY 3 Divers bring food and medicine to the boys.

JULY 4 The team are taught how to use a diving mask and equipment.

JULY 8 The rescue begins. Four boys are brought out of the cave.

JULY 9 Four more boys are rescued.

JULY 10 The last four boys and coach are rescued.

CRYSTAL CAVES

Crystals grow in caves when water heated by **molten** rock, or **magma**, floods the cave. When the liquid cools, the minerals dissolved in the water form solid crystals. This is called crystallization.

Crystals line the walls of Mlynki Cave in Ukraine.

The Cave of Crystals in Mexico contains giant crystal pillars and sits just 1 mile (1.6 km) above a pool of **magma**. This keeps it so hot that people can only survive inside for about half an hour.

DID YOU KNOW?

A geode is a hollow rock filled with crystals. Most fit in the palm of your hand, but the Crystal Cave in Ohio is a huge geode that people can stand up inside.

crystal pillar

WHAT ARE CRYSTALS?
Crystals are solid objects made up of tiny parts called **molecules** that fit together in a repeating pattern. Did you know that salt, sugar, and snowflakes are all crystals?

snowflake, or snow crystal

Crystals found inside an old mine in Slovakia.

Wieliczka Salt Mine in Poland is carved from one of the world's best-known crystals—salt. People have mined salt there since the 13th century. Today, tourists visit to see its many statues made of salt.

FAMOUS CAVES: ŠKOCJAN CAVES

Filled with waterfalls and lakes, Škocjan Caves in Slovenia are giant canyons shaped by an underground river. The caves are home to some rare animals.

rimstone pools

Thundering waterfalls flow into lakes inside the caves.

Water flowing down slopes inside the caves created rock formations known as rimstone pools. These pools look like stairs.

The huge Pipe Organ is one of the biggest **stalactite** formations in the caves.

One of the giant canyons is called the Murmuring Cave. It gets its name from the **echo** of the river flowing below.

The blind cave salamander, or olm, is just one of the rare creatures living in these caves. It hunts for food using its other senses and can live past 100!

VOLCANIC CAVES

Volcanic **eruptions** create caves when rivers of **lava** cool and harden at the surface, creating tunnels beneath them. These caves are known as **lava** tubes. Caves can also form from the **erosion** of volcanic rock that cooled millions of years ago.

Fingal's Cave in Scotland is made from the **erosion** of volcanic rock. About 60 million years ago, a giant **lava** flow cooled slowly and evenly, cracking into six-sided hexagonal columns. Over thousands of years, waves crashing against these columns carved out a volcanic sea cave.

The Giant's Causeway in Northern Ireland formed in the same way as Fingal's Cave. The names of both the cave and causeway are thought to refer to Fionn mac Cumhaill, a heroic giant from Irish myths.

HOW LAVA TUBES FORM

1 Liquid **lava** flows downhill in a stream.

2 The **lava** starts to cool and harden into rock at the edges.

3 A solid crust forms over the top of the stream, creating a tube shape.

4 The **eruption** ends, and **molten lava** drains out of the tube, leaving behind a tunnel.

About 3,000 years ago, a volcanic **eruption** on Lanzarote in the Canary Islands created the Cueva de los Verdes **Lava** Tube.

LAVACICLES

As **lava** cools, it can drip from the ceiling of the tube and harden into lavacicles. These lavacicles are in the world's longest **lava** tube—Kazumura Cave in Hawaii.

CAVE CITIES

Long ago, many people lived in caves. The remains of their underground homes give us clues to what life was like in the past. Some people, known as **troglodytes**, still live in caves today. The caves' thick walls keep out both extreme heat and cold winds.

ANCIENT ART

Cave paintings show us what **prehistoric** life was like. Paintings on the walls of France's Lascaux Caves show the animals that lived there about 17,000 years ago.

Pueblo people in Colorado carved these homes into sandstone between 1190 and 1260. Fewer than 100 years later, they abandoned the site. The reasons why are still a mystery to scientists.

Sassi di Matera in Italy is a network of ancient cave homes and one of the world's oldest cities. People still live there today, and some of the caves are vacation homes.

MOVIE-STAR CAVES

In Matmata, Tunisia, modern **troglodytes** dig large pits and carve out cave homes around the edges. Movie fans know Matmata as the home of Luke Skywalker in *Star Wars*.

These cave homes in Cappadocia, Turkey, are sometimes known as fairy chimneys.

Some modern **troglodytes** live in Kandovan cave city in Iran. They carved their homes into cone-shaped pillars of volcanic rock.

LIFE IN THE DARK

Caves may look dark and creepy to us, but they make perfect homes for many animals. Creatures that live in caves are called **troglobionts**.

BATS

During the day, many bats roost quietly inside caves. At night, they swoop out, making high-pitched sounds. They find food by listening for the **echoes** of their sounds bouncing off **prey**. This process is called echolocation.

SPIDERS

Female European cave spiders weave nests and attach them to cave ceilings near the entrances. When the spiderlings hatch, they follow the light outside and leave the cave to find new homes.

sighted tetra

FISH

Over millions of years, Mexican tetra fish **evolved** into two groups. The fish that live above ground have good eyesight, while the cave fish are blind. These blind tetras move around cave rivers by sensing pressure changes in the water.

blind tetra

SNAKES

Ridley's beauty snakes are also called cave racers because they race up cave walls and munch on roosting bats. This useful way of catching dinner means the snakes never have to leave their underground lairs.

FAMOUS CAVES:
WAITOMO CAVES

Glowing lights cover the walls and ceilings of Waitomo Caves in New Zealand. This star-like display is made by a tiny insect called a glowworm.

READY, SET, GLOW

New Zealand's glowworms emit a blue-green light known as **bioluminescence**. They set up traps made of sticky silk threads. They then use their glowing lights to lure in flying insects for their dinner.

DID YOU KNOW?

Local Māori people were the first to know about the caves. The name Waitomo comes from two Māori words—*wai*, meaning water, and *tomo*, meaning hole.

EXPLORE THE CAVES

Visitors can take a boat ride or even sit on rubber rings and go black-water rafting through the caves. Glowworms don't like noise, so people must sit quietly to watch the insects light up.

ANCIENT INSECTS

Glowworms aren't the only creatures that lurk inside these caverns. Cave wetas belong to a group of insects that have been around for millions of years. They were alive even before the first dinosaurs!

CAVE ADVENTURES

Caves can be fun places to explore, from scuba diving to ice climbing, and from camping to rafting.

Scuba divers and snorkelers flock to Mexico's Yucatan Peninsula to explore thousands of **cenotes**. These natural sinkholes are filled with sparkling clear water.

Cenote El Pit, Mexico

Tourists float on big rubber rings down an underground river that runs through Pindul Cave in Indonesia.

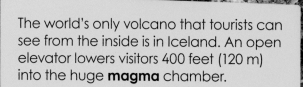

The world's only volcano that tourists can see from the inside is in Iceland. An open elevator lowers visitors 400 feet (120 m) into the huge **magma** chamber.

Guides on Matanuska **Glacier** in Alaska teach beginners to ice climb inside glistening **glacier** caves.

Cave explorers can camp overnight in Hang En Cave in Vietnam. The campsite is the first stop on a four-day trek through underground rivers and rainforests.

SUPER SOUNDS

A hard, flat surface reflects sound just like a mirror reflects light. Some cave walls reflect sounds so well that we hear them repeated back as **echoes**. Many caves have amazing **acoustics** because of these **echoes**.

HOW ECHOES WORK

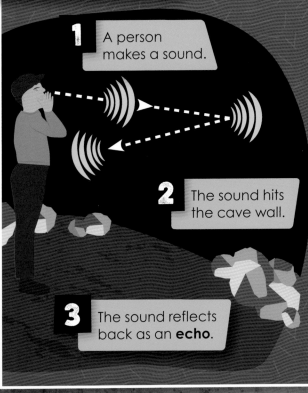

1 A person makes a sound.

2 The sound hits the cave wall.

3 The sound reflects back as an **echo**.

Fingal's Cave in Scotland is also known as The Cave of Music. Once inside, visitors hear **echoes** of waves crashing against the rocks. When the German composer Felix Mendelssohn visited in 1829, these **acoustics** led him to write a piece of music—*The Hebrides*.

Drach Caves on the island of Majorca in Spain are the stage for an underground concert. Visitors watch from the dark shore as musicians play in lit-up rowboats.

The ocean carved this cave in Norway over thousands of years. Today, it is known as Ocean's Cathedral. Once a year, during the Traena Music Festival, crowds and musicians fill the cave with sound.

The inside walls of the human-made Barabar Caves in India are polished as smooth as glass. This creates **echoes** so long and loud they drown out peoples' voices before they can say a whole sentence.

CAVE SCIENCE

Scientists carry out important research in caves. Discoveries made deep underground can help cave experts understand Earth's **climate**, how to build safer cities, and even how to improve modern medicine.

These blind cave salamanders can survive for up to 10 years without food. Scientists think that studying them may reveal how humans can survive starvation.

blind cave salamander

This narrow cave in Death Valley, Nevada, hides clues to 500,000 years of **climate** history. This may help scientists predict future **climate** changes.

Scientists have found **bacteria** deep in the Lechuguilla Caves in New Mexico that cannot be killed with antibiotic medicines. Studying these **bacteria** and other tiny living things in the cave may help us find new ways to treat illnesses.

crystal **stalactites**

sinkhole

When water erodes rock below ground, the surface can cave in, creating a sinkhole. Some sinkholes are so deep they can swallow cars or houses. Scientists study them to figure out where future sinkholes might occur so lives and buildings can be saved.

VISIT A COOL CAVE

Have you ever been inside a cave? Maybe you could explore one near you, but don't go inside without a guide. Some caves run tours for visitors—they are called show caves.

A child explores a Russian ice cave.

Bermuda's Crystal Cave is filled with **stalactites** and a clear underground lake. Guides take visitors across floating paths, where they can peer down at rock formations in the water.

stalactites

Children can go on fossil-hunting tours in the Jenolan Caves in Australia. Guides help them carry out experiments, learn about ancient animal bones, and hunt for treasure.

The Great Stalacpipe Organ inside Luray Caverns, Virginia, is one of the world's largest musical instruments. During cave tours, the organ plays music by gently tapping **stalactites** with rubber mallets.

witch-shaped **stalagmite**

Spelunkers can explore eight different caverns at Wookey Hole, England's biggest show caves. One cavern is named the Witch's Kitchen after the witch-shaped **stalagmite** inside.

MAKE YOUR OWN CAVE

Make a cave home for your favorite toy. Follow these instructions and have fun.

1 Ask an adult to blow up the balloon.

2 Tear the newspaper into short strips. Mix the craft glue and water in a bowl with a spoon.

3 Use a paintbrush to add the glue mixture to the top half of the balloon. Then place a layer of paper strips over the glue. Let the paper dry, and then add more glue mixture to the dry paper. Place another layer of paper strips on the glue. Repeat this process 3 or 4 times, letting the paper dry between each layer.

4 Leave it for a day or more, until dry. Then pop the balloon. Cut a door in your papier-mâché cave, and trim the base so it sits flat.

5 Paint your cave. You can also add your own cave paintings.

6 When the paint is dry, the cave home is ready for your favorite toy.

GLOSSARY

acoustics how the walls, roof, or other surfaces in a place affect the sounds within it

bacteria tiny living things with only one or a few cells. Some cause illnesses and others keep us healthy.

bioluminescence a light or glow made by a living thing

cenote a deep natural well or sinkhole that forms when a cave roof collapses

climate the usual weather conditions of a place

echo the repeated sound heard when sound waves bounce back from a hard, flat surface

eolian cave a cave carved out of rock by the wind

erosion the slow wearing away of rock by wind, water, or ice

eruption a natural event during which lava, ash, and dust burst out of a volcano

evolve to change slowly and naturally over a long period of time

extinct no longer found alive; died out